# The Year Of Living Gratefully

## A Remarkable Way To Make Your Child Happier And More Grateful

**Sandra Tisiot**
*Creator of My Life Locker™*

**FEATURING THE**
*HGG© System*

Published by **Sandra Tisiot**

Copyright © 2015 **Sandra Tisiot**

ISBN: 978-0-9865607-1-2 (book)
ISBN: 978-0-9865607-2-9 (digital)

**Book Cover Design:**
Yannis Souris / www.creativemarketing.com

**Book Formatting:**
Helena Guzmán / www.helenaguzman.com

# CONTENTS

# DEDICATION

I dedicate this book to my son, my greatest HGG.

# PREFACE

**_The Year of Living Gratefully_ provides easy-to-implement guidance on making your children happier and more grateful**

How do you teach your children to be more grateful? To be happier? To recognize the greatness of life all around them?

As the mother of an only child, author and business woman Sandra Tisiot wanted her son to know that life did not revolve solely around him. And so after lifelong research – reading whatever she could get her hands on, talking to other parents, formulating ideas – she brought together her thoughts and instincts to create something both brilliant and simple.

The author introduces in _The Year of Living Gratefully_ what she calls _The HGG© System_: a way to help make her son – or any parent's child, for that matter – happier, more grateful, and more aware of how great life can be. _HGG_ involves a short daily ritual that focuses on three simple questions:

- _What was your happy thought for the day?_
- _What were you grateful for?_
- _What was great about your day?_

Sandra Tisiot knew that creating and planning a program was one thing. Successfully putting it into practice was quite another. Then communicating it to other parents was, again, something altogether different. And so she embarked on a journey with her son to turn thoughts into action into results. And she wrote a book about it – the book you're holding right now.

*The Year of Living Gratefully* is more than an account of Sandra Tisiot's one-year journey to give her son the means to live a happier and more grateful life. It is also an instructional guide any parent can start today that will bring lifelong benefits to their children. As a bonus, parents are finding it's making them happier and more grateful too.

Through simple and practical daily rituals, any parent can begin using *The HGG© System* right away.

Reading the book will not take a long time, but the positive results for you and your children will last a lifetime.

## PRAISE FOR *THE YEAR OF LIVING GRATEFULLY:*

*"What a brilliant idea. A ton of value here for families. Easy to understand and implement. A great read."*

— **Kathie Donovan, author/television host**

*"A good balance between showing and instructing without it feeling like an insurmountable challenge for parents. It reads well, flows smoothly, and integrates the psychological theory effortlessly."*

— **Natalia McPhedran, Author, *Life With Kids***

# 1  THE BEGINNING

Harlen was sitting up in bed, resting his head against a pillow and ready to talk when I came into his room at bedtime. He looked at me and smiled – the sweet grin of a sleepy eight-year-old boy – and I smiled back.

"So tell me about your day," I asked, sitting down next to my son and stroking his head.

"I was just thinking today was better than I first thought," he said.

Harlen looked around his bedroom at the colourful range of toys, games and art, then ended his sweep of the room by looking into my eyes.

"I'm very thankful – very, very, very thankful – that you got me all the stuff in my room," he said. "And I'm thankful for everything you've given me, Mom."

My heart swelled with pride and love hearing this from my sweet young son. He wasn't just talking about the material things he'd been given. His appreciation and gratitude was going deeper than that. He was transforming from a typically self-centred eight-year-old into a grateful child. And in just six months. The change had been so dramatic, so positive. I could feel tears of joy welling up in my eyes when Harlen brought me back to the present.

"And I'm thankful for Odie," he said.

I couldn't help but smile broadly at this. Odie is our dog, a happy Yorkshire Terrier we adopted at four months old from a couple living in an apartment. We gave him a home in our house and a backyard to run freely.

"We've had him for three years, and you're just thanking me now," I said.

"Well, it took me a while to be thankful," he said.

I felt like I was glowing inside. It's working. It's definitely working. Harlen is truly becoming a happier, more grateful young boy.

◆

## Say hello to Harlen

Our nightly ritual had been going on for six months at this point. But it was far more than just asking "How was your day?" on day one and having my son immediately express all that he was thankful for.

It wasn't quite that simple.

To begin, I'll offer a little background.

I am a single mother to Harlen, whose name I've changed for reasons of privacy. As I'd mentioned, my son was eight years old when all this began. Harlen had started school when he was just three years old. Young, I know, but he was ready, and I was too. I chose to send him to a Montessori school.

For those of you unfamiliar with Montessori education, here's a brief online introduction from a school website:

*Dr. Maria Montessori, Italy's first female physician, created a revolution in childhood education with her Montessori Method. A basic Montessori tenet is that a child learns best in an environment that supports the individual and offers appropriate materials and guidance for each stage of development. Advocating the "whole child approach," Dr. Montessori's goal was to provide a program in which the child flourishes intellectually, physically, socially, emotionally and spiritually.*

I will never forget the day Harlen came home one day in his final year at Montessori and told me his *happy thought.* "Happy thought," I remember saying to myself. "What a fabulous idea!" And so I tried to ask him every day what his *happy thought* was for that day.

When Harlen left Montessori after three years there, I was a little distracted by the demands grade one at his public school was putting on him – had he finished all his work? – and I lost the habit of what had become our happy thought routine. It wasn't until a few years later that I appreciated what a positive ritual it was – and is – and that I should keep it up.

## The beginnings of our journey

I have always been an avid reader, always interested in self-discovery and self-improvement. I had been reading a wide range of books on mysticism and the divine from the time I was 19, and had travelled as far as India to study these topics deeply.

In India, and elsewhere, I continued my dance studies. Dance, for me, was my meditation. It never let me down and, at times, I have felt it saved me. Yet it was always this calling to a spiritual and grateful life that I knew was guiding me. A life I wished to share with Harlen. At the same time, I did not want to feel I was programming him with any of my views. I understood how important it was for him to develop on his own at his own pace.

As I studied and learned more while Harlen was still young, I did not want to feel he was being at all left behind on our lifelong journey as mother and son.

But I was unsure how to start. I had so much to learn myself. My education may have truly begun that day I decided my boy and I had to learn these new things alongside one another.

He was still new to the world, just as I was still new to being a mother. So my plan was that we would learn together and from one another. This would be a journey for both of us.

I recognized these lessons could only begin at home. They were a gift I wanted to bestow upon my son. What I didn't – couldn't – realize at the time was that these lessons were also a gift he gave to me. I became a better mother and my little miracle would, I hoped, become the best little boy he could possibly be.

Taking this journey together has been a wonderful decision. While I have been able to impart the wisdom of my experience to my son, he has reminded me of rules and lessons long forgotten. Memories not experienced since I was a child.

## Creating good habits that last a lifetime

The lessons we were to learn had to be applied continuously and consistently in order for them to stick, for us to keep them going.

Like a lot of people, throughout the course of my life I have formed new good habits and moved on with life healthier and happier. I'd think, "It's all good." Then I might slack off a little and, in the blink of an eye, the good habit was gone. How did that happen?

I have learned after many miscues the importance of choosing lifelong habits and sticking to them faithfully. Sure, you could bend a little here and there, but if you let more than a week go by, you'll likely have to start all over again. Not fun! Starting over rarely is.

From my research into the science of habits, I've learned that psychologists tell us that up to 90% of all behaviour is habitual. What we do repeatedly become our habits. Habits are a series of decisions over time. If you do something daily, it becomes part of your routine.

I've always heard about the *21-day rule* – that it takes 21 days to form a habit. After reading James Clear's article on how long it actually takes to form a habit (see jamesclear. com/new-habit), I learned the origins of the 21-day rule – or should I say, the 21-day myth.

In 1960, American cosmetic surgeon and author Dr. Maxwell Maltz wrote in his preface to *Psycho-Cybernetics: A New Way to Get More Living out of Life* that his patients took a minimum of 21 days before adjusting to their new face. From there, the 21-day rule took off, as readers of the bestselling book misinterpreted the notion of *habituation* – how long it takes to get used to something – as being the same as habit formation.

More rigorous recent research, including a 2009 study led by Phillippa Lally at University College London, showed it took, on average, 66 days to form a habit, and that individual results could vary anywhere from 18 to 254 days. Quite a spread.

So, simply put, I would offer that a habit is formed when it becomes a daily process, or a regular part of your life. Problem is, many good habits so easily stop after just a short time.

To help build habits, I really like James Clear's 3 Rs of habit change: Reminder, Routine, Reward. (Read about them at jamesclear.com/three-steps-habit-change.)

For Harlen and I, our *Reminder* was bedtime. Our ritual became part of our nightly bedtime *Routine* and our *Reward* was seeing each other smile. A happy kiss goodnight. Grateful dreams ahead.

With the journey my son and I were embarking on, the goal was to create a lifelong habit; a change in thought pattern that would last long after the appeal of something new and shiny had faded.

Yes, a habit requires constant commitment. And I suggest it is truly formed when you start having feelings of guilt should you alter, change, or omit it.

I don't claim to be a guru on how to develop and maintain good habits. And I certainly don't have the answers to all of life's questions. But I have assembled a few keys to forming good habits that I think are very valuable. And I believe my job – or maybe my calling in life – is to pass on what I have learned.

## Creating better kids through developing better habits

We all want our children to develop basic good habits – brush your teeth, wash your face, eat with your mouth closed – that will stay with them all their lives. This is not a book about instilling good habits such as these.

As a parent, one of the primary complaints I hear is that our kids are ungrateful. They complain, enjoy a sense of entitlement, and have no patience. Theirs is the *me* generation that desires instant gratification. With so many technological conveniences they sometimes forget the small things in life to be thankful for.

As an only child, my son always received a lot of attention. In fact, he got pretty much all my attention. He was never what I would consider a bad child, but he could act self-centered and selfish. He expected a lot and was not as calm or as helpful as I would have liked him to be.

## The power of the positive

I did not then, nor do I now, ever focus on the negative. I have always wanted Harlen to care and appreciate more outside of himself. To possess a higher level of awareness. For this awareness, I believe in the need to focus on the positive.

If, like me you have only one child, you might realize you tend to centre your world around him or her. I was okay with that, in fact I loved it, but I realized that it could cause a little imbalance or an overindulgent child. I wanted a kind-hearted kid who not only had a good sense of self, but had a great sense of others as well. In helping him become grateful, I thought I could achieve that.

While much of the time Harlen was a good kid, I knew he could be more. I wanted him to be a gratitude junkie. He had to come to understand it for himself, to create his own habits, but I was going to be his coach.

I had to show the way. I showed him that I wrote in a gratitude journal every morning. I would shout out my gratefulness during the day: *"Oh, I am grateful for my leg not hurting as much! …. I am grateful for the garden flourishing! …. I am grateful for my business – I was really busy today!"* And so on. And then of course, for our bedtime routine, I led the way with our gratitude statements.

## Teaching Harlen to be HGG

What's HGG?

If you've flipped through this book's pages, you may have seen HGG without an accompanying explanation. HGG, in a nutshell, is absolutely central to *The Year of Living Gratefully*. It's integral to the creation of gratitude.

HGG stands for *Happy, Grateful & Great.*

I have read many books in the vein of developing an "attitude of gratitude," and how to harness that energy. While this is important for adults, it is even more imperative for children.

For the journey Harlen and I were embarking on, I had to go deeper beyond the regular "please" and "thank you" of good manners. So I created my own ritual, a system, which I call *HGG: Happy, Grateful & Great.*

Each night when tucking Harlen into bed, I would sit with him and ask him to tell me three things:

- *What was your happy thought for the day?*
- *What were you grateful for?*
- *What was great about your day?*

Then I, in turn, would tell him my happy thought for the day. What I was grateful for. And what was great about my day.

That's how HGG began.

Our special routine became a very relaxed time for us, with our sharing creating a calm and safe environment where he felt he could tell me anything.

This book details a year of that nightly ritual. A ritual I believe has been fundamental in helping my son Harlen become a grateful young boy. A ritual I hope helps make him a grateful person his entire life.

At this point, I do want to be clear about my intentions. I am not saying this is something you have to do with your children if you want them to become more grateful.

I am simply telling my story – the story of my son Harlen and me. I found a practical, simple solution that worked for me. A nightly ritual that's helping Harlen become HGG: Happy, Grateful, and Great.

My hope is that HGG can work for you too.

◆

## 2    THE RITUAL

### Bedtime is the time to talk HGG

It became a regular evening ritual for us. At the very end of our day, after Harlen was in bed, he and I would "HGG", as we began to call it.

We'd tell each other what we were happy about and grateful for, and what was great (sometimes even just "good") about our day.

Over time, this nightly ritual created a wonderful bond between us. A special, often magical connection achieved through thinking and sharing – and repetition.

### HGG became the most important part of our day

HGG not only became an important ritual for my son and me; it also became the most important part of our day.

If my son couldn't think of anything – which occurred more regularly when we first began HGG – then and only then would I offer suggestions.

I would talk about what I saw in his day, prompting him to recognize HGG moments. Each time it became easier for him to recognize HGG moments on his own. With each night, he became more comfortable with the ritual. Any prompting became less and less necessary.

Having established the routine, I need only sit by his bed and look at him with love, and he knows this is the cue to start.

## Both parent and child learn a lot

Doing HGG taught Harlen the power of his thoughts, and how these positive thoughts could guide his attitude and feelings. I wanted him to begin recognizing the good in even the smallest thing. As we practiced the nightly ritual it became easier for him to think with fluidity. Through engagement and repetition, it no longer became a challenge for him.

I learned a lot as well. For starters, I learned to delight in the enchantment that is part of a child's life.

I learned not to create barriers. And to be very careful not to criticize (as much as I might want to). This was Harlen's story, not mine. I had to accept his words as is.

## The importance of ending the day on a positive note

Sometimes it is difficult to maintain the ritual because if I am tired, all I want to do is give my son a big kiss, say good night and head to bed.

But I don't. I try not to deny him this very important time. These are the most important moments of the day.

Just before you close your eyes, I believe it is vital our thoughts be positive and happy. We deal with enough negativity as it is. We all encounter negative situations in one form or another throughout our day, so sending my boy (and myself) off to sleep with only positive thoughts has become paramount.

Going to bed with peace and tranquility in our minds, drifting off to sleep having wonderful reflections, is a great way to end the day.

## Expect a less-than-smooth start

It didn't go exceptionally well in the beginning.

At first, I didn't document these special times, as I thought it would be too impersonal. And it turned out it was. If I wrote anything down, took notes, Harlen looked at me a little funny as if to say, "Mom what are you doing?"

Later on, when he understood better and was more comfortable with HGG, I asked him if I could write while he was talking. He told me that was okay. I further explained to him that we were writing a book together, sharing our thoughts and our stories. He was completely fine with that as well.

## How you might get your HGG ball rolling

Through your own gratitude statements, you can help guide your child's HGG by example.

Parent statements, for example, might be as simple as these:

- I am happy to see you treat the dog so nicely and take it for walks.
- I am so grateful when you and your friends get along so well during play dates.
- I really thought it was great that you made a healthy snack choice today.
- I am happy to see you had so much fun playing baseball today.

THE YEAR OF LIVING GRATEFULLY

- I was grateful that you brought your plate to the kitchen after dinner.
- I really appreciate the kindness you showed your grandmother. It was great to see you do that.

Gratitude statements like these help your child recognize that small actions can make their parents – and others – happy.

As a parent, you don't have to say things like, "Be kind to your grandmother." If you are thankful for what occurred, your child soon learns it is a really good thing.

These types of gratitude statements help children recognize the good in most everything. They learn their choices have an impact on other people's feelings. They can make others feel good – and they possess the power to do that. In turn, this helps make them feel good about themselves.

## HGG lets kids feel grateful for whatever comes to mind

HGG is kind of like a game for kids; it's fun. Most importantly, HGG is a huge self-esteem builder. Kids realize they can be grateful for anything that comes to mind.

At first, Harlen was grateful for a LEGO toy he received. Later, he was grateful for a warm day, a beautiful flower, having fun at baseball, or for a safe flight we took. Simple things that most children take for granted.

## Don't be surprised to see a more observant child

Harlen was getting to the point where he could more easily point out what happened during the day. Things that would normally slip his mind.

My child was becoming incredibly observant of even the smallest things. Details that pretty much everyone else would ignore because they didn't even see them. Harlen saw them. My pride in him and his powers of observation were growing exponentially with each passing day.

I loved watching the transformation. But, like anything else, you have to keep it going if you want it to work. Habits can break down so easily, even if we've spent a long time establishing them.

Children will often do as you do. Occasionally Harlen would ask me first – "Mom, what's your HGG?" – even before I sat by his bed. I would smile, thinking that, "Yes, he's got it. I am so grateful he's having fun with it."

◆

## 3   THE JOURNEY

### Expect a slow start

Looking back to where we started, and seeing where Harlen and I are now, I'm reminded of that classic quote attributed to the Chinese philosopher Laozi:

*A journey of a thousand miles begins with a single step.*

At first, before HGG was truly established, the journey was more about teaching and giving Harlen examples, then letting him explore what that meant to him.

I nudged, prodded, offered examples, told my own sometimes elaborate stories before he connected to what this ritual was all about.

It was a slow start. A sometimes rocky start. At first he could think of nothing nor remember anything about his day. He needed to be reminded.

During these early days and weeks and months, I kept at it. Persistence, I reminded myself, is key. Even if Harlen couldn't always express what he was happy about, what he was grateful for, what was great about his day, he at least was hearing all of my positive HGG thoughts.

Early on, as I have mentioned, I didn't write down Harlen's thoughts. I wanted him to better understand what we were doing with HGG. I wanted him to feel comfortable with the process.

Then…

# Some snapshots after six months of HGG

## HGG: Thursday, May 10

Harlen: "I am grateful you pushed me to go to baseball, because I struck out four batters and I had a great hit."

He smiled.

What a moment this was for me.

First off, pushing is never fun and can be quite exhausting, but sometimes it's needed. And to know that your efforts are recognized brings great joy. I am HGG to have witnessed this in my son.

Later, in the kitchen:

Harlen: "Mom, I am really grateful that you are trying new recipes, but can I have some mac and cheese."

## HGG: Tuesday, May 22

Today was a breakthrough. I realized Harlen's awareness was growing dramatically. HGG was working.

We just got home after spending five days in Tampa with my then partner. There was a long, unplanned day of travelling, as our second flight was delayed. Finally home and very tired, we were ready for sleep; it was well past Harlen's usual bedtime.

All I wanted then was for my head to hit the pillow, but I couldn't. I had made a promise to my son and to myself. These are the times when I realize I have started something and must be persistent. I must be the example... always a good example.

As we were getting ready for bed, Harlen said, "Mom, you're not selfish." I wondered where this was coming from.

"Yes, you're right. I'm not. Thank you," I replied, not wanting to push for an explanation, but very curious. I wanted him to keep going.

Harlen continued, "You didn't buy anything."

"Well, I guess I didn't need anything," I responded. He was referring to our shopping trip in Tampa. The intention was for it to be a "carte blanche" trip: buy anything you want.

He saw that I didn't just go ahead and do that, even though I could. Harlen nodded. He realized that just because you can do something, it doesn't mean you should, or have to.

Then, as I sat by his bed, he said, "I put my rocks away." He had put the five gemstones we bought at LEGOLAND on his shelf, along with his other rocks. He asked me to get him the pink one. He held it, rubbing its smooth surface, then said, "I am grateful for our safe flights from Tampa to Philadelphia and from Philadelphia to Ottawa."

I smiled. I thought he was going to be grateful for all the LEGO he got (he had been spoiled at LEGOLAND). But something changed. He was grateful for our safe flights. Yes, his awareness was growing. It was growing in leaps and bounds.

## HGG: Wednesday, May 23

Harlen: "I'm very thankful – very, very, very thankful – that you got me all the stuff in my room, and that I got to go to LEGOLAND, and thankful for everything you've given me. And I'm thankful for Odie." (Odie is our dog, a Yorkshire Terrier.)

"We've had him for three years, and you're just thanking me now," I said.

"Well, it took me a while to be thankful," he replied. "He is such a good dog."

I just grinned at this, and felt like I was glowing inside; it's definitely working.

Harlen continued, telling me that he was thankful for his Dad and half-brother coming over and playing basketball with him. And then, again, how really thankful he was for all his stuff.

## HGG: Thursday, May 24

Thursday night after baseball Harlen is tired and worn out. It was a long game, as he pitched a lot. After eating some cereal because he needed a snack, he's not sure what he feels more: hunger or exhaustion. He chooses exhaustion, but decides to eat first, then sleep. I wanted to lie down as well.

We went to his room, and I was just about to tell him we could skip tonight's HGG and follow up in the morning. But no, something has changed.

"Mom, HGG."

I realized he was starting to look forward to his nightly HGG. You can't imagine how wonderful that was for me – and ultimately for both of us.

I let him speak. He reviewed his day and recognizes the good things that happened. The habit is formed.  It has worked, and for that I am HGG.

## Precious Moments

It is still surprising to me when my son pauses in our front garden and appreciates the flowers, commenting on how he likes the roses or the hostas or the peonies.

It makes me smile; he is appreciating so much that enters his field of vision and is seemingly missing nothing.

Who would ever think that a child – not just my child, any child – really would stop and smells the roses?! Harlen was not just learning the importance of being aware and appreciative of the beauty in this world. He was living it.

## HGG: Wednesday, May 30

Harlen couldn't think of anything to be grateful for, and he asked me for help - An opportunity for us to talk and share. After school he had walked to the corner store, about six blocks away from our home, but he didn't tell me what happened until bedtime. He saved it until then, but was eager to tell me when the time came.

He told me there was a boy sitting on the front step of a house, and he suddenly flashed something at Harlen. It looked like a gun, and the boy asked Harlen if he knew what it was. Harlen shrugged and guessed a Nerf gun. Then another boy appeared from inside the house and told the first boy to take Harlen's money. Fortunately Harlen just kept on walking, but the threat affected him so much that he teared up, and when he arrived at the store it was obvious something was wrong. Luckily, we know the owners, and they gave him a chocolate bar and walked him home.

On the way back, the owner asked him if he was having a tough day, and Harlen told him about the boys at the house and how their threatening words made him very nervous. "They were bullies," Harlen said, "and I didn't like that".

Why didn't he say something to me right away when he got home? My HGG for that day was very simple. I told him I was so grateful that nothing had happened to him.

He said the incident had scared him. I told him I understood, and I asked him what we could learn from it. I suggested a few things: walk and don't talk; walk with someone; bring a phone and call me. He just said that he didn't think he would go back that way again. I proposed that he should try to go back, but this time I would go with him.

So it was that our HGG time was also turning into our sharing time.

## Lessons to be learned

One of the hardest things I've had to deal with as a parent is my son's extremely competitive nature, and how to manage those "less than triumphant" moments. I have tried a lot of approaches, including these:

- Stay positive.
- Tomorrow will be better.
- You learn from your mistakes.
- You can't always win.
- Everyone needs a chance.
- It will get better.
- You'll get better.
- You're learning.

But Harlen didn't really begin to understand until we found the following way of looking at things:

Each moment that is not good prepares us for the moments that are good. Therefore, having a bad game really allows us to appreciate the good game. Having a bad throw allows us to be grateful for the good ones.

I saw the lesson in full action again when Harlen hurt his left wrist at school. He was annoyed by it, but then said, "Well, I'm grateful it's not my right wrist... my pitching hand".

So a simple mantra was born: "I am grateful today for (insert lesson)."

For example, "I am grateful today that the other team caught my pop fly, because now I know to either hit low into the infield or farther into the outfield."

## HGG: Monday, June 4

I started with my HGG tonight. "I am grateful for my massage, and that you were so good when I left you with your brother and asked you to take care of the dog, and you did."

Harlen: "I am grateful for you letting me play my video games, and also for you leaving me with Manuel and making me responsible. I let Odie out and everything was good. I am grateful for Odie, and happy he is around. He is my friend."

## HGG: Tuesday, June 5

Last night we went to bed late because the next day was a teacher's professional development day, so Harlen had the day off school. I thought maybe it would be a quick goodnight HGG, but no, not this night.

"Mom, are you coming?" he said from his bed, ready to tell me what he was grateful for.

"I had a great game tonight at baseball," he said. And he really did: pitching, hitting, throwing. He was really "on" tonight. He was grinning as he continued. I could see him thinking about the rest of his day, scanning his mind for memories.

How many times have parents asked their children how their day was, or what they did? Only to hear, "I don't know." Or just "Fine." They can't remember, or don't want to talk about it. Or, worse, they don't care to.

Well, Harlen thought about it, and said, "I really liked that we had science in school today, and I learned that I was the best one in science in our class. I knew the most. I was HGG for that."

## HGG: Tuesday, June 12

Harlen had another good night at baseball; he was smiling and "up." We picked up some groceries on the way home. He enjoyed his coconut chocolate bar, and he shared half with me. I was grateful for that; I so love coconut, but loved more that he wanted to share it with me. After a shower and dinner it was off to bed. The regular routine: brush teeth, let the dog out.

Harlen: "Mom… HGG."

"Yup, I'm coming."

HGG had become a habit – a good habit. No, a great habit, an established routine. I no longer had to ask, he just gave. He wanted to. I would simply look into his eyes, smile and listen. He would share, smile and feel grateful.

I can't tell you what was going on in his head. Can anyone truly say they know their children's every thought? Though I believe we understand a lot, I mostly rely on what I hear and see. Observation and listening are very powerful tools.

I was very grateful that night for Harlen's baseball coach, because he was teaching the kids how to just be the best they can be, whatever that is. Kudos to him. See? You don't really have to know someone to be grateful for what they've brought to your, or your child's life.

## Contemplations and more lessons learned

I wondered how I would I handle the HGG evenings if I had several children.

What a great family ritual it could be. Each family member could take a turn until everyone had a chance to go through his or her individual HGG thoughts first.

In addition to learning about gratitude, they would learn respect. They would know to listen to whoever was speaking without interruption. This lively family discussion group would not only be educational and inspirational, but a bonding experience as well.

Listening is crucial, and listening without judgment is critical. It's an art that has been lost by many, but so easy to achieve.

## HGG: Wednesday, June 13

Now, all I need to do is look at Harlen intently and smile, and he knows that it is that time: HGG time.

Harlen: "Okay, my HGG for today is the play-date with Massi, playing Skylanders, and learning a new song on the guitar."

## HGG: Thursday, June 14

I tell Harlen about how thankful I am for my chiropractic treatments and for feeling great. He thought about his day but couldn't think of anything, so instead he said, "You know, tonight my HGG is this: I am thankful for my mom, dad, brother, and sister; for water; for food; and for my toys." Then he grabbed and kissed our dog.

Wow, I couldn't stop smiling. Those were his thoughts as he went to sleep. It was beyond working. He was already my best little boy, but he was rapidly becoming the most grateful little boy. I don't think it was possible for me to have been more proud.

Earlier, he had heard someone talking about guardian angels. "I have one," he said. "His name is Jonas." (Jonas was a friend who passed away when Harlen was three months old.)

"Yes," I said. "And you are very lucky to have him. I feel blessed knowing that Jonas is still with us in this way. I am truly grateful for that."

## HGG: Sunday, June 17

Harlen: "I am grateful for playing baseball well, even though we did not win. I am happy I had fun this weekend. I finished my homework, and I am happy that we didn't have so much homework this year."

## HGG: Tuesday, June 19

Tonight's dinner was not the greatest, I'll admit. I tried a new recipe and added more salt than I should have. I don't use much salt as a rule, so even a little extra was too much for Harlen.

He came to me and said, "Mom, I really appreciate what you did, but there's too much salt."

I just smiled. I didn't care about the food, only that he was continuing on his journey to appreciation and gratitude.

## HGG: Thursday, June 21

Tonight, Harlen's HGG was, "I'm glad my Mom has a sense of humor".

## HGG: Friday, June 22

I was tired tonight and just felt like putting Harlen to bed and going to bed myself, but he wouldn't have it. "No Mom," he said, "we have to do HGG." Every day his personal growth was becoming more and more remarkable.

## HGG: Monday, June 25

At school my son suffered a head injury. I went to get him, and learned he had been pushed by another student and had fallen backward on the steel play structure. It was quite a hit, and he was cut and bleeding. He was also dizzy, and I immediately thought concussion. I decided to monitor him closely, and if he didn't recover quickly I would take him to my athletic therapist.

That afternoon, I did what every Mom would do: I spoiled my child, took care of him, loved him.

That evening he said his HGG: "I am grateful that you took care of me, Mom. Thanks."

## HGG: Tuesday, July 3

After the school year, I like to take Harlen away for a week – a kind of reward for getting through the school year. So off we went to Tampa, where my partner at the time was living.

My notes from the time reveal that I continued an abbreviated form of HGG for Harlen, and continued my own journaling. Though we were home in a sense, we were still on holiday, and it's always harder to maintain a ritual when you are on vacation.

The first night I hugged him very hard and told him how much I loved him, and that I was so thankful that my men were together. I felt HGG for everything. Harlen was grateful we were there in Tampa too. He said, "I am grateful for everything I have. Everything is great. I have fun and I'm grateful for it all.

And so our HGG ritual continued on throughout the summer.

## HGG: Tuesday, September 4

A new school year has begun and a new chapter of HGG.

As I was sitting with Harlen on his bed, I felt ill and exhausted. I had been suffering from vertigo/concussion since March, and so some nights I needed to get to bed promptly. This night I could really feel the discomfort in my neck.

"Mom, we haven't done HGG," Harlen said.

"OK, it's all good" I replied. "You start."

"Well, I'm glad we had baseball practice."

This seems normal now, but since practice had been two days earlier, it meant his recollections were expanding. Then he continued, "I'm glad I went to Tomas's for a play-date. Um, I mean, hangout session." My boy's perceptions of his activities were changing, and if we hadn't been doing this ritual for so long, it's something I might have missed.

## HGG: Wednesday, October 3

Harlen's H – for Happy: "I'm happy I made the soccer team. I got a new book for my report."

His first G – for Grateful: "I'm grateful for water."

His other G – for Great: "I went to guitar, and I'm getting better. And Mom was grateful that she had finally discovered that the wall behind my bed was not so clean, so she cleaned it up. It was my booger wall."

Harlen and I laughed and laughed so hard at that. When we laugh together it's not mere giggles or chuckles, it's extreme, full-on hilarity.

## HGG at midday

Sometimes I will throw HGG into the middle of our day. I'll say, "Oh, I know what my HGG is going to be tonight. It's this moment; I am truly grateful for…" And I'll say whatever it might be.

For example, today it was this: "I really appreciated you coming to the grocery store with me today. It was so nice having help with the cart and having you put the groceries on the belt and then in the car and putting the cart away. Your help felt huge to me. These are chores I have to do myself every week, sometimes more, and it is really cool to do it with you."

He smiled. Maybe he thought I was crazy. I asked him, "Any idea what yours will be?" And he replied, "I'm doing mine tonight" – which made me smile right back at him.

Later that night, I also I tell Harlen that I really appreciate that he ate all his breakfast and put his plate in the dishwasher.

## HGG: Wednesday, October 24

A particularly poignant and memorable HGG from my son: "I am blessed to have a mother like you."

## HGG: Wednesday, November 28

I just got home from a conference clear across the country. Harlen said he was glad I was back, and happy that I'd had a safe flight.

His HGG was about his Minecraft game, his friend's birthday party, and that he got two goals and two assists in his hockey game.

How HGG has changed for us – and changed us

I particularly notice this night how our time for HGG has evolved and expanded. It's become more than specific details about what we're happy about, what we're grateful for, what was great about our day.

It's also about what happens next, as Harlen just keeps talking and, more importantly, sharing his feelings. In these comfortable, relaxing times he tells me stories, and I sit and listen, smiling and glowing. I love our time together. I tell him I love him, and he tells me the same.

◆

## HGG: Sunday, December 2

Harlen: "We lost. That's not HGG. I didn't do anything good."

I helped him to refocus and remember.

Harlen again: "I did well at hockey, Andrej came, and that was fun."

"What are you happy for?" I asked.

"I don't know," he replied.

"Think."

"I'm happy for both those things. The happy and grateful was that Andrej came, and the great was that I did well in hockey.

"Do other families do this?" he asked.

"Yes, they do – but differently, I suspect. Maybe some do the same… or only partly. My wish is that you and I can share our journey and by doing so, everyone can start to do HGG the way we do."

## HGG: Tuesday, December 4

I said, "I'm grateful that my neck pain has subsided, and for the love of family and friends." And I was so grateful for the hug Harlen gave me yesterday.

Harlen: "I don't know… Did I tell you I am grateful for you getting hot chocolate for me?"

I needed him to dig a little deeper, so I asked if I could help.

He said yes with a smile on his face.

"How about this?" I said. "I am grateful that after my shower my Mom gave me extra Minecraft time."

His eyes lit up. "Oh yeah!" he said. I got him to repeat it so he could feel it.

## HGG: Wednesday, December 5

It was a tough night. I had just found out that my 24-year-old niece had died. I was sobbing, and Harlen came over and hugged me without saying a word. Not for just a short moment, but longer. I hugged him back and told him how much I loved him. I could feel his kindness.

## HGG: Wednesday, Dec 12

I was telling a friend that Harlen had asked how long we were going to do HGG, and I had told him "forever," and how I thought this had overwhelmed him. My friend recommended taking a break, and I thought that was a good idea.

◆

## A break from the HGG ritual

I explained to Harlen that we were taking a break from HGG. He seemed hesitant but said okay.

Tonight I sat by his bed and he just talked. He asked me a question about his friend and I answered honestly, as I always have.

Then, when he continued talking, it hit me: This was it. He was confiding in me, telling me what he thought, how he felt. We were really connecting. This was *our* time. The moments that connected us through HGG still existed by our talking together. And I couldn't have been happier.

## HGG: Monday, December 17

I asked Harlen if he missed HGG. He did, and wanted to start it up again. Break over.

◆

## HGG: Thursday, December 20

Over Christmas break, we celebrated early with my partner in Florida. We told Harlen he'd really like to get Harlen something he really wanted and this time it could be big. Harlen selected two toys that were still pretty modest. On the plane home he talked about another toy that he was also eying and I asked why he didn't get it. He replied that he didn't want to be greedy.

## HGG: Tuesday, December 25

As I watched my son open his Christmas presents ¬– he loved LEGO and received a few larger ones, as well as his first phone – I was so proud of the gratitude that he expressed.

"Thank you, Mom."

"Thank you, this is great."

"Wow, thanks."

It was music to my ears.

I realize all kids are grateful for their presents at Christmas, but it was the deepness of his thanks that was so apparent to me.

## HGG: Friday, December 28

Harlen had some friends over playing video games. When a third boy arrived, I let him into the game room and heard laughter and cheers. Then I overheard Harlen say, "Okay, so let's finish here and then give Tomas a turn."

This was nice to hear because it was not so long ago that I had to gently – okay, maybe not always so gently – remind Harlen that when he had friends over, everyone got a turn at the game. While fairness and equality had not always been uppermost in his mind, it was gratifying to see my son was seeing their importance – even without any reminders from me.

## HGG: Monday, December 31

I asked Harlen what he was grateful for in the past year. He didn't hesitate or need to think it over. "I am grateful for getting good at hockey this year," he said. "I am grateful that my Mom and I are working on HGG together. I am grateful for my life."

I was grateful for that too.

What better way to remember the year than with gratitude?

◆

## A full year of living gratefully comes to a close

While I hadn't strictly adhered to a day-in and day-out January 1 to December 31 program, I knew that my one-year HGG journey with Harlen was winding down.

And I now knew without a doubt that HGG was working: My son Harlen was a more grateful, more aware, more appreciative and – dare I say it – a truly happier young person.

HGG had worked. And it would continue to work.

As with all parenting, there were still challenges ahead. I knew I had guided Harlen down the right path, and that I must continue to be his example.

Harlen's half-sister Dominique visited us over the holidays. She attends university in another city, so she doesn't get to see him much. But after spending time with her little brother, she told me she saw a big shift in him: he was kinder, more caring. Everything wasn't just about him. And he was grateful...

My intention was to teach Harlen that we are more than just ourselves. We should strive not to be self-centered and selfish, but to be kinder. More aware of others and their feelings. Considerate of our environment. Helpful. Mindful. Grateful.

And he is learning. This process never ceases. It is a lifelong journey, an ongoing recognition of what it is that makes us happy, makes us grateful, makes our days great.

It is a journey that Harlen and I simply call *HGG*. A journey I hope that you and your children might share. Perhaps starting today – and for years to come.

# 4   INTEGRATING HGG INTO YOUR LIFE

## Some Dos And Don'ts of HGG

There is no right or wrong on how an HGG practice might unfold in your household, but there are some fundamental dos and don'ts to follow for HGG to work well. I offer what I feel are important here.

## The Dos

- Complete the practice at bedtime. (Remember, this does not have to take long. Let it just unfold. One day might only be one minute while another lingers on for 10 to 15 minutes.)
- Offer an easy-going, safe, quiet time.
- Be prepared to be a great listener.
- Wear a warm smile.
- Make eye contact.
- Let your child finish what they are saying – right to the end.
- Start with small HGG moments and work your way up to larger, more complex ideas and issues.
- Show respect.
- Repeat, repeat, repeat. Every night. (We're developing a habit, so keeping to it every night is very important.)

## What if your child has nothing to say?

- Go first. Tell them what you are happy about, what you are grateful for and what was great about your day. Start with small stuff, show them the way. If they are still having trouble, offer to suggest what you saw about their day that they may be HGG for.

- Keep it simple until they "get it."

- Touch upon something that is memorable for them.

- If your child refuses to play along, one tip that might work is to keep sharing your HGG moments. Tell your child how grateful you are that they simply listened.

## The Don'ts

- Don't set a time limit.
- Don't interrupt.
- Don't judge.
- Don't question.
- Don't remark.
- Don't attach previous beliefs to the process.
- Don't miss the next night if you have to miss one.

## Other important don'ts:

- If you are upset with your child, don't lash out.

- If you are angry, stay patient.

If your child has done something you don't agree with – wait. Wait for the opportunity during HGG time to deal with it. For example, your child may not have called you to tell you where they were and then arrived home late. You were worried, upset and rightfully so.

During HGG you could offer, "I am so grateful when you're at a friend's house that you call me and let me know what time you are coming home." You might also say: "It worries parents when they don't know where their children are. It's not a nice feeling." Or "I am so grateful you are always safe and when you let me know you are." Or "I am so happy to see your face when you get home. It feels really great knowing I have raised such a responsible child".

Parenting is a tough job and I praise each and every parent out there.

Just stay patient and trust that this practice works. Before you know it, HGG will become a fun and vital part of your day.

◆

# 5   BEYOND THAT YEAR'S JOURNEY

When I've told friends about HGG, they have responded with something like, "Oh, that sounds great!"

They'd often ask me if they could use it in their own lives. "It doesn't belong to me," I would tell them.

Of course, it should be shared; that's what I had hoped for. That's why I've written this – and why you're reading it now.

## The positive psychological effects of HGG

At bedtime – or any time of the day, for that matter – HGG moments allow us to truly connect with things we love and those we love.

HGG moments instantly bring your mind directly to positive things.  And it was extremely important to me that my son's last thoughts before drifting off to sleep and into his dream state were positive. A child sleeps better, has happy thoughts, wakes up happier and is generally happier through the day if the last thoughts before going to sleep are positive ones.

Psychology has long known the effects of the dream state and how it adjusts the chemistry of the body and mind, influencing the health of our total being.

In Psychology Today, science writer Susan Reynolds and neuroscientific researcher Teresa Aubele, Ph.D., co-wrote that "Thinking positive, happy, hopeful, optimistic, joyful thoughts decreases cortisol and produces serotonin, which creates a sense of well-being. This helps your brain function at peak capacity."

## The joys and benefits of sharing HGG

Creating the HGG ritual was a great joy for me, not only for the transformation in my son, but also because we had created something together. HGG would not have happened, it would not exist without him.

After we took a break near the end of our yearlong journey, I asked him if he wanted to continue, and he responded with an enthusiastic "Yes!" I believe he enjoyed the sharing. But also, of greater significance to me, he missed our time.

After one year of HGG, Harlen became almost a gratitude machine. He could easily reflect and, within those reflections, generate positive thoughts, expressed as gratitude. It was clearly apparent to me he now held values that were kinder, more thoughtful, more mindful.

HGG worked for us, and it can work for you and your family. It doesn't matter if you have one child or seven, everyone – parents and children – have the opportunity to say what they are grateful for. When everyone listens, everyone benefits.

## An attitude of gratitude

Together, Harlen and I created an attitude of gratitude through HGG – three little letters my son will remember forever.

And this is just the beginning. How I love my son, and while to me, he's the best little boy in the world, I know I have shown him the path to be a great student, a great sportsman, a great worker in whatever he chooses, a great partner to whomever he ultimately choose to spend his life with – as the years bring those things to him.

Whatever, wherever, however he spends his life, these lessons will stay with him and show him that he can always be grateful for even the smallest things. He knows how to do this now, so there's no telling what he can bring to the world when he becomes a man. But for now – right now – he's continuing to build gratitude.

The power of gratitude is the power of positive. How can you be – or remain – negative or sad when you're happy, grateful and great?

## Overcoming sadness through gratitude

Of course, sadness and misfortune, frustration and disappointment are part of life. Into each life some rain must fall – as the poetry of Longfellow and the popular song from the 1940s remind us.

Just after the third year of living gratefully I had begun sharing with Harlen, I had to deal with a very sad time in my life. The breakup of a relationship is never easy. I was tearful during this time and often showed Harlen my tears. I showed him I was vulnerable; we all are. I was embracing my sad moments, but a child is not yet equipped to understand and manage his own emotions. Children are taught by our actions.

As we approached HGG during these times, it was difficult for me. However, I shared my gratitude about my journey, not my sadness, and he looked at me with surprise. He didn't know how to comprehend my sadness now that I was giving it gratitude. By filling my heart with gratitude I healed my pain.

Partly because of the state I was in, I can't recall precisely Harlen's HGG at that time. I had been strong and resolute for him, but now HGG was for me. I had come full circle; HGG was helping me heal.

I kept hearing the words of writer Rhonda Byrne, author of *The Secret*:

> "Be grateful for what you have now. As you begin to think about all the things in your life you are grateful for, you will be amazed at the never ending thoughts that come back to you of more things to be grateful for. You have to make a start, and then the law of attraction will receive those grateful thoughts and give you more just like them."

Hard as it was, I kept up my gratitude journal. I had seen gratitude in action, how it worked, and I knew it would help me with this – like it had with everything else.

I continue to be grateful, and see its manifestations every day in ways small and large.

## The value of engagement and encouragement

As a parent, you need to continually engage, encourage, spend time, and show the way.

When I've told my friends I've been writing a book to help moms and dads around the world with their kids, Harlen has sometimes offered his concise summary: "You mean HGG!" My friends will look puzzled, and ask what it is, then listen and nod when I explain the basics of HGG: sharing Happy, Grateful, and Great moments.

I have never expected miracles or major transformations, but what I did hope for, and still do, is kindness, recognition of things beyond you, and being thankful for everything. Even the little things, because they add up.

It's a bit like taking inventory, evaluating even the small accomplishments, or stocking shelves. One by one, you put things on the shelves, and before you know it you're all stocked up.

## HGG sparks ongoing communication

The conversation that comes as a result of HGG is especially important. The continuing communication. The stories I get to hear. The experiences Harlen is excited about – even if it's a video game I really don't understand at all. He was – and is – getting it: Stay focused on the positive and positive things will happen.

You may remember hearing your parents say things like, "When we were young, we used to walk to school in eight feet of snow." Or, "When I was young, we used to play outside from dawn to dusk – when we weren't helping our parents with chores."

Well, it dawned on me that someday my son would say to his kids, "When I was young, your grandmother and I used to do HGG every single day."

He would remember, but more, he would carry on the ritual, the tradition. He's not perfect, nor am I, but we are perfect as we are and our journey is about trying for our own excellence. Be excellent in all you do and you will do excellent.

I may or may not be around to see my grandkids, but I know, I am certain, if there are any, Harlen will tell them stories about our ritual.  In fact, I cannot even think or write about it without a good cry.

## An ongoing legacy of positivity

We all want to teach our kids in a positive way, and leave them with a small legacy of ours. We want the best for them, and this was my part on how I tried to do my best for him.

Every day I have been witness to HGG in action. It really is the small stuff, but that will lead to a big person in the future.

For my son and I, HGG has become our code for reminding ourselves about the good stuff, that we could find the good in everything without it becoming a chore.

For my final words here, I leave you with the opening lines from a wonderful poem titled "On Children" by Kahlil Gibran:

*Your children are not your children.*

*They are the sons and daughters of Life's longing for itself.*

*They come through you but not from you,*

*And though they are with you yet they belong not to you.*

I wish you great success in your life and in the lives of your children. And I sincerely hope that HGG becomes a positive part of your lives.

◆

SANDRA TISIOT

# ACKNOWLEDGEMENTS

In thanking those who made this little book possible, I would like to offer up my own personal HGG:

## What is my happy thought for this book?

Knowing that other parents will see positive results for their children after they read this book and put what they've learned into practice – that has been a real source of motivation and inspiration for me.

## What am I grateful for in writing this book?

My gratefulness extends to many things, but I'll boil it down to three:

- *Taking this wonderful journey with my son Harlen.*
- *Setting out to write this book – and achieving my goal.*
- *Receiving the support of my family and friends.*

## What is great about this book?

It's complete – I've pushed it like a boat out into the world – but what places this book goes now, I don't know. Not knowing – the possibilities, the potential, the mysteries – is part of what, for me, has made the creation of this book great. It's a bit like raising our own kids: you do your best, then set them off to make their own way in the world.

I believe this book will help you – and all readers. Even if you never take a single step toward implementing the HGG© System into your children's lives (if you, in fact, have children), I feel you can still get a lot out of reading this book. In truth, I believe everyone can and will take away something positive from this book. Which I think is a great thought. I hope you think so too.

*– Sandra Tisiot*

# ABOUT SANDRA

Sandra was born in Hamilton, Ontario. After high school her passion for dancing brought her to California where she fulfilled her childhood dreams by performing with various professional dance troupes. There she also received her BA in Dance and Business from California State University of Long Beach. An unfortunate injury prevented her from continuing to dance professionally, but it didn't dampen her spirits or her love for dancing and performing. Continuing her education back East in Washington DC, she ultimately received her MA from the American University.

Sandra's talents have taken her to many cities throughout North America and around the world where she has achieved much acclaim for her skills and insight in writing and teaching in the Arts world and the business world.

Relocating to Ottawa Canada in the early 90s to be closer to family was yet another fortuitous step for Sandra. She has made an indelible mark in the financial sector in both the sales and management side of the mortgage industry by achieving top sales recognition with all four companies she worked with.

Sandra spends her spare time continuing her passion for dance by teaching BARRE fitness classes. She enjoys reading, writing, and spending quality time with her family and her friends. By constantly thinking of new ways to help people, she created, *MyLifeLocker*, an organizational workbook where families can find peace-of-mind knowing all their life information is on one-spot.

Sandra is also the co-founder of *Suits-Me.ca*, a charity that collects clothing for the Women's Mental Health Program at The Royal in Ottawa. She raises funds for this cause through her annual *WomenInBusiness Conference* where she brings in acclaimed speakers to inspire, motivate and nourish women in all aspects of their lives.

Sandra is currently enrolled in a PhD program in Metaphysics at the University of Sedona where her gratitude journey continues.

# MY HGG NOTES

www.ingramcontent.com/pod-product-compliance
Lightning Source LLC
Chambersburg PA
CBHW051046030426
42339CB00006B/225